Down on the Farm

COWS

Hannah Ray

🌳 Crabtree Publishing Company

www.crabtreebooks.com

Published by Crabtree Publishing Company
Copyright © 2008
www.crabtreebooks.com

PMB16A
350 Fifth Ave., Suite 3308
New York, NY 10118

616 Welland Ave.
St. Catharines, Ontario
L2M 5V6

First published in hardcover in the U.S.A. in 2006 by QEB Publishing, Inc.

Cataloging-in-Publication data is available at the Library of Congress.

ISBN 10: 0-7787-4051-X paperback
ISBN 13: 978-0-7787-4051-3 paperback

Printed and bound in China

Written by Hannah Ray
Designed by Liz Wiffen
Consultant Sally Morgan
Editor Paul Manning
Picture Researcher Joanne Forrest Smith
Illustrated by Chris Davidson

Publisher Steve Evans
Editorial Director Jean Coppendale
Art Director Zeta Davies

Picture credits

Key: t = top, b = bottom, c = center, l = left, r = right, FC = front cover

Alamy Peter Dean 7, /David R Frazier Photolibrary.Inc. 13, /Lynn Stone 16b; **Corbis** Adrian Arbib 15, /William Gottlieb 13, /Earl & Nazima Kowall 18, /Brian Vikander 17t; **Ecoscene** Peter Cairns 16t; **FLPA** Ray Bird 8t, /Nigel Cattlin 12, /Peter Dean 17b, /Mitsuaki Iwago 4; **Getty Images** 14br, /Lisa Adams 6, /Gordon Clayton 8b, /Lester Lefkowitz 11, /Reneé Lynn 9, /James Martin 19, /Mecky FC, title page, /Tim Platt 14t; **Still Pictures** Chlaus Lotscher 5

CONTENTS

Words in **bold** can be found in the Glossary on page 22.

Why we need cows

Do you know where milk comes from?
Or the shoes you wear on your feet?
Where do we get the meat to make tasty
hamburgers? All these things come from cows.

4

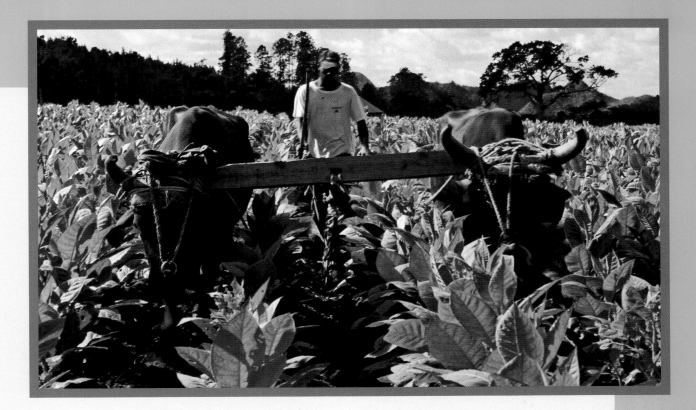

Cows working in the fields on a Caribbean island.

Cows are very important animals. They give us milk, leather, and meat. In some countries, cows work in the fields, pulling **plows** to break up the soil. Then the farmer can plant crops such as **wheat** and **corn**.

Cows from nose to tail

Cows are big animals. A full-grown cow is about five feet (1.5 m) tall and weighs around 1,300 pounds (600 kg). That's the same as 30 six-year-old children!

Tail to flick away flies

Thick skin covered in hair

Eyes

Ears

Nose

Mouth

Udder to store milk (female cows only)

Hooves

This cow wears a bell so the farmer can hear her if she strays.

6

FARM FACT
Cows use their long tongues to wrap around stems of grass and weeds to pull them out of the ground.

Height of cow

Height of six-year-old child

Each day a cow spends eight to ten hours just eating grass.

7

It's a cow's life...

This cow has a baby cow, or **calf**, inside her. Before the baby is born, it has to grow inside its mother for nine months.

The first milk the mother feeds her calf is special. It helps the calf grow big and strong.

When the calf is about a week old, the farmer will start to feed it **hay** or **grain**.

At six months, the calf will eat grass in a field with other cows.

At about two years, the female calf can have a baby of its own.

Most cows live for about twelve years.

These baby calves are about ten weeks old.

9

Moo chew

A cow's stomach is very special.
Your stomach has only one main part,
but a cow's stomach has four!

Parts of the stomach where the cud is stored

Parts of the stomach where the cud is digested

1 When a cow eats grass, it chews
it just enough to make it easy to swallow.
The partly chewed grass, or **cud**, is stored
in the first two parts of the cow's stomach.

FARM FACT
A cow's stomach can hold up to 60 gallons (227 liters) of partly digested food. That's enough to fill a small wading pool!

2 When the first two parts of the cow's stomach are full, the cud comes up from the stomach to the cow's mouth to be chewed again.

3 After the cud has been chewed some more, it goes to the third and fourth parts of the cow's stomach, where it is **digested**. Some of this digested food goes to the udder, where it is made into milk.

11

From cow to carton

These cows are being milked by machine in a **milking parlor**. Using modern machines, farmers can milk more than 100 cows per hour. In some countries, farmers still milk their cows by hand.

A tanker takes the milk to a **dairy** where it is heated up until it is very hot to kill any germs. Once the milk has cooled down, it is safe to drink. The milk is then put into cartons or plastic containers, ready to go to the stores.

FARM FACT
Female cows cannot make milk until they have had a baby calf. Farmers milk each cow twice a day.

13

Why raise cows?

Not all cows are raised for milk. Many cows are raised for their meat. Meat from a cow is called beef.

The beef in hamburgers comes from cows.

The cow's skin can also be made into leather. Leather is used to make shoes, bags, belts, and furniture.

FARM FACT
Gardeners often spread cow manure on the soil to help plants to grow. Cow manure can also be used as **fuel**.

Even cow **manure** has its uses. This African tribeswoman is using cow manure mixed with grass and twigs to build a hut. When the mixture is dry, it will be as strong as cement.

In Tibet, herdsmen build walls out of cow manure to protect their tents from the wind.

15

Cow cousins

Many different types of cows can be found all over the world.

HIGHLAND

These cows are from Scotland. They are famous for their long shaggy hair and curved horns.

TEXAS LONGHORN

These large cows with extra-long horns were brought to the United States by the Spanish over 500 years ago.

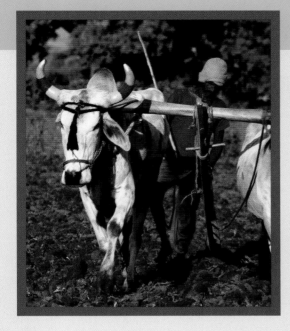

INDU-BRAZILIAN

These cows have the biggest ears of any type of cow. They live in hot countries such as Brazil.

POLLED HEREFORD

This is a very old type of British cow. The word "polled" means hornless.

17

Cow customs

INDIA

In India, cows are **sacred** and must not be killed or hurt. Sacred cows are even allowed to wander through busy city streets full of traffic!

SWITZERLAND

Every year, Swiss people celebrate when the cows return to the mountain grasses. There are feasts with music and **yodeling** contests.

AFRICA

In many parts of Africa, cows are used instead of money. If a man from the Masai tribe wants to get married, it will cost him a lot of cows. He may have to give his bride's father 30 cows.

FARM FACT
In India and Nepal it is good luck to give a cow a snack, such as a piece of bread or fruit, to eat.

A Masai bride in traditional wedding costume.

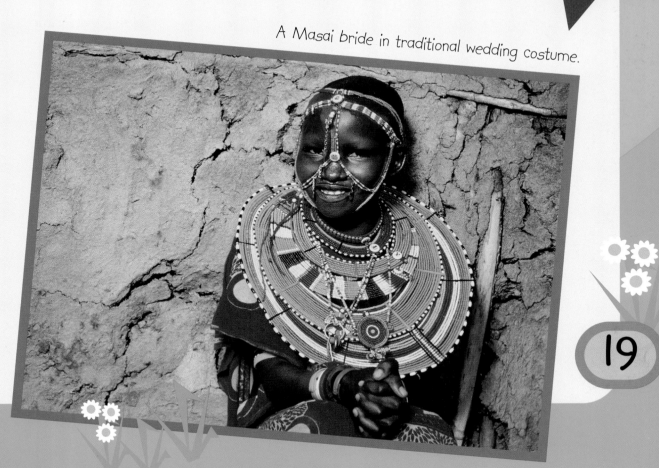

19

Farmyard fun

Milk from cows is used to make butter, cheese, yogurt, and chocolate. You can make your own butter. Just follow these steps:

1 Pour the cream from some whole milk into a clean jelly jar with a lid.

2 Screw the lid onto the jelly jar. Make sure the lid is on tight.

3 Shake the jelly jar up and down.

4 Keep shaking...

FARM FACT
It takes roughly 10 cups of milk to make 5 ounces (150 g) of butter—the amount you need to make a birthday cake!

5 Shake some more... You will see butter start to appear on the surface of the cream.

6 When you have made enough butter, use a plastic knife to spread it onto a slice of bread. Some people like to add a little salt to their butter.

21

Glossary and Index

calf a baby cow

corn a plant grown for its yellow grains that are used as food

cud partly chewed grass that is stored in the cow's stomach and chewed again before being digested

dairy a place where milk is heated to kill germs and put into containers or cartons

digested when food is broken down so that the body can use it for energy

fuel something that is burned to make heat or energy

grain the seeds of cereal plants such as wheat

hay cut and dried grass used to feed animals

manure smelly brown waste produced by cows

milking parlor place where cows are milked

plow farm machine used to break up soil and make fields ready for planting

sacred especially important or holy

udder part of a cow where milk is made and stored

wheat a plant grown for its grains that are used to make flour

yodeling type of musical call used in Switzerland

22

23

Ideas for teachers and parents

- Make a poster to show how milk finds its way from the cow to the home. Ask the children to illustrate each stage in the process.

- Make a cow collage. Draw an outline of a cow on a large piece of paper. Have fun looking through magazines and newspapers and cutting out cow-related pictures. Look out for scraps of cow print material and any other odds and ends to liven up the children's pictures. Fill in the cow outline by sticking on the items that you have collected.

- Research different breeds and make fact sheets on the children's favorite breeds. Some cows look amazing!

- With the children, find out why milk is good for you. What does it contain? What parts of the body does it benefit?

- Challenge the children to think of stories, jokes, and rhymes featuring cows, for example, "Hey Diddle Diddle" and "Jack and the Beanstalk."

- See who can spot the most cows on a car or bus ride. Can you identify the breeds?

- If possible, visit a farm where children can see real live cows.

- Make a Highland cow mask. Cut eye holes out of a paper plate and draw on a big cow nose. Add some wooly bangs and stick on ears and horns. Make holes on each side of the plate and add elastic so the mask can be worn.

- Make a simple wordsearch using cow-related vocabulary from this book.

- Visit **www.moomilk.com** for a fun and accessible website giving more information about the dairy industry and cows. **www.highlandtoffee.com** is a bright, activity-packed website about Toffee, the Highland cow. Children can read stories, color in pictures on screen, and play a variety of games.

PLEASE NOTE
- Website information is correct at time of going to press. The publishers cannot accept liability for links or information found on third-party websites.
- The activity on pages 20–21 is not suitable for children with an intolerance to dairy products.

24